50 Powerful Date Ideas

Brag-Worthy, Cost-Effective Dates From A Professional Dating Coach

By Jordan Gray

Relationship Coach at
www.jordangrayconsulting.com

September 2014

ISBN: 150235053X
ISBN-13: 978-1502350534

Table of Contents

Why I Wrote This Book

Do you ever wish you could be more romantic and charming? Would you like to earn fast bragging points with your partner without excessive effort? That's where this book comes in.

Each one of the dates within this book had to meet three major criteria before being considered. It had to be 1) powerful; 2) time-efficient; and 3) cost-effective. If the date did not meet all three criteria, it was filtered out. So if you're expecting to see the type of typical dates that a search engine would suggest (e.g., dinner and a movie) then you are reading the wrong book.

This book is a reference guide. There is nothing to memorize in this book. This will be a secret weapon that you can keep on your phone/computer and use to continuously WOW your partner.

Whether you're taking her on the first date, the fifth date, or the 500th date, this book has you covered.

Who Am I?

My name is Jordan Gray and I am a relationship coach. I empower people to get into (and stay in) thriving relationships. I've helped people across several continents, showing them how to develop fulfilling and lasting connections with their partners.

And in my own life, I have gone on hundreds (if not thousands) of dates. Through my years of effort to become the best partner possible, I have discovered some of the most consistently powerful dates... and I can't wait to share them with you! I personally guarantee that, if you use even a fraction of what you find contained within this book, you will be able to build more romance, spontaneity, and connection into your relationship - no matter what stage it's in.

Date Ground Rules

There are a few guidelines that you should know and implement to make sure that all of your dates go off without a hitch. For those of you in long-term relationships, these points are mainly for newer relationships so feel free to skip ahead to the "Date Disclaimer" if you'd like (although you can definitely still learn something new here).

I've always loved these guidelines because they are so 'set-it-and-forget-it,' it's ridiculous. And as we all know, the more prepared you feel going into a date, the more you can relax and truly be yourself.

And, as a side note, although I am writing this book primarily to my heterosexual male audience, this book will be just as valuable to any other readers. So read on!

- Always Be Leading

"The number one most important thing about a perfect date is his effort in creating it. Have a plan. As a woman, I can put up with a certain amount of 'So what do you wanna do...' conversations, but I would really rather not." – Kiran, 24

Women are attracted to a man that has the ability to lead them. The fact that you sought out this book means that, on some level, you're intuitively aware of this (way to go!) and that you want to be seen as a leader in your relationship. Having the ability to tell your date/girlfriend/wife that you are planning something and she should leave her Friday night open will give you major bonus points. Whether it's the first date or fiftieth date, women will always be disappointed if they get picked up for a date and the man asks, "So what do you feel like doing tonight?" Please don't ever be that guy! Be the man that has a plan and lead her on an adventure.

- Built-In Exit Strategy

Having an exit strategy is important for different reasons in different relationships. It all comes down to remaining flexible. If you're on a first date with a woman, and it turns out you don't actually get along that well, then being locked into a three-hour dinner would be a nightmare. On the other hand, if you're on a date with your long-term partner and it just so happens that she is suddenly struck with the overwhelming urge to rip your clothes off and jump you, who are you to deny her that right?

- Ready-To-Use Conversation Pieces

Why do all of the heavy lifting yourself? This book is all about making your dates feel effortless. Many of the dates in this book have built-in conversational pieces around you so that there are things to talk about/laugh at/enjoy together.

- Physical Touch

Finally, these dates have lots of opportunities for physical contact between the two of you. What is the difference between your date and everyone else in your life? Physical intimacy and sexual tension. There's nothing worse than being on a dinner date where you sit opposite your date, staring each other down while slurping your spaghetti noodles. This date gives you effectively ZERO chance for physical contact unless you both happen to reach for a bread roll at the same moment. (Romantic? Uh… I think not.) So feel free to shape these dates to allow for as much physical contact as possible (including sitting next to her rather than opposite her).

How To Treat Her On A Date

Women want to be treated well. Women want to feel appreciated. The most common mistake I see guys making (especially in the early dating stages) is setting up a beautiful evening but then treating the date like an old friend. By the end of the night, the woman leaves feeling confused ("That's weird; I *thought* he asked me out on a date…") and the man leaves feeling frustrated ("Why didn't I get closer to her? We didn't even kiss… I *totally* blew it!"). Let's assume that if your date put on make-up, spent at least half an hour deciding what to wear, and showed up to spend time with you, she's into you. Assume attraction and treat her like a woman. Make her feel safe, sexy, and surprised and you will undoubtedly be placed in her "Best Date Ever" category.

Who Should Pay?

Ah, yes, the age-old question.

Social norms have noticeably shifted these past few decades. In the 1950s, the gender gap was very rigid. Men did manly things and woman did girly things. Through the sexual revolution of the 1970s, there was a backlash against gender norms. Women flexed their masculinity by burning their bras and taking on careers outside of the home. Men let their hair grow long, learned how to cry, and expressed their softer feminine side. Post hippie era, we now live in a healthier grey-zone where men and women alike are free to express their masculine and feminine sides. You might be thinking, "This is all well and good, but what do we do about the payment issue?"

In my opinion, it currently lies somewhere between 'the man should still pay' and 'whoever initiates the date should pay.' Call me old-fashioned, but I think chivalry is far from dead. And though it may be gasping its final breaths, being chivalrous and covering the bill makes it that much easier to stand out from other men.

Additionally, if you really knew what women spent on things like their hair, makeup, and wardrobe, you wouldn't hesitate for a second to pick up that tab. (Hint: our underwear is $10 for a 3-pack, and they have pairs that are $50+…)

From my past decade of full-time dating, I have found that women really only care about one thing when it comes to handling payment: don't let it cause awkwardness.

Did you read that? It bears repeating.

Don't let the bill cause any awkwardness!

In other words, you're in a bad way if the check comes at the end of your delicious meal and you both are doing the awkward payment dance. You start to feel each other out, to see who is offering to pay… Or maybe you're just going to split the bill? Or maybe not? Just avoid all of that horrible mess with these easy tips.

1) Don't let it hit the table

The golden rule for avoiding awkwardness, hands down. If you're going to a place that isn't really that expensive (which you won't be when you continue to follow this guide), use your ninja-stealth to hand your server a credit card on your way to the bathroom. Ask for the bill to be prepared. Then, when you're done in the bathroom, come on out, sign the bill and be on your merry little way back to the table. Check? What check?

2) Don't take her up on her offer of splitting it

Whether it's a token offer or a real one, insist that because you wanted to take *her* on the date, you would only feel right being able to treat her to the evening. Oftentimes, the woman will reach for her purse (even when she knows the bill has been fully paid) with an "Oh, you shouldn't have" expression on her face and say that she wanted to pitch in. This is very sweet and can be a sign of a quality woman. But nine times out of ten, don't take the bait. She is usually just being polite. However, exceptions do apply...

3) If she really insists or you can tell it makes her feel uncomfortable...

Some women in this modern era really aren't comfortable feeling indebted to others (especially new partners). Call it a lack of trust or a surplus of social conditioning to be independent, but some of your dates will just not be into it… and that's totally fine. One way to handle this objection is something that I have used many times to set up the second date. If you have been having fun up until this point and you know you want to see each other again, ask her if she cooks. If she says yes, tell her that she can make you dinner for the next date. This is wonderful because it allows her to feel like the pressure has been taken off and it also lets her gift you back with a (generally) less expensive date. Win-win!

What Women Really Want From A Date

"It's about connection in the end. The images that come to mind when I think back to some of my best dates are eye-contact, laughter, intelligent conversation and heart-stopping sexual chemistry." – Jen, 27

It's a common mistake that men make, assuming that women want the exact same things out of a date (especially the first few dates). Men believe that women need to be impressed. They think they want to be lavished with gifts and fancy dinners. But, when you ask most quality women how they would feel if a man spent a lot of money on them on their first date, they describe feelings of awkwardness, discomfort, and obligation.

Think about it this way…

Women want your presence, not your presents.

Women are MUCH more impressed by a genuine emotional connection with a confident man than by a weak emotional connection with a guy that pulls out all of the stops on the first date. So stop trying to be impressive. Start allowing your dates to have the time and pacing necessary for connection to occur.

There are many ideas for dates in this book. Use them wisely and use them slowly. Fight the urge to pile one on top of another to create a six-hour super-date. Easy does it.

Date Disclaimer

Before I get into the list, I want you to be mindful of one thing. Some of these dates will speak more to you than others; that's fine. You do not have to use all of these dates nor should you use them all in a row.

You'll notice that each date is rated on a scale of one to five on five different parameters (physical intimacy potential, emotional intimacy potential, conversational ease, cost effective, and brag-worthiness). Different relationships generally require different ratings in regards to these parameters. For example, if you are going on a first date with someone, I recommend choosing dates that rate highly on conversational ease and emotional intimacy potential. If you are already in a long-term relationship then I would suggest prioritizing brag-worthiness and physical intimacy potential. The rest is up to you.

The Five Level Date Decoder

Physical Intimacy Potential

This parameter is all about the likelihood that physical touch will occur within the date's structure. The traditional "dinner date" would score an emphatic ZERO if it were being rated because two people sitting across from each other at a restaurant have very little chance for physical contact. Contrast that with dates like partnered salsa lessons or a home-spa date where you massage each other, and you'll see why this parameter is so necessary to consider.

It bears repeating- dates that score highly on physical intimacy potential are generally better left to the long-term relationships. A five out of five for physical intimacy potential is a date too presumptuous for most first dates.

Emotional Intimacy Potential

Emotional intimacy potential speaks to the likelihood that you and your date will form or deepen your emotional connection with each other. Many of the activity dates and romantic date structures score highly on this parameter.

Conversational Ease

For those of you who don't want to do all of the heavy lifting conversationally, this parameter will let you know if a date does most of the talking for you. Going for a hike, doing karaoke, or seeing a live comedy show are all dates that would score highly on conversational ease.

Conversely, if you are totally confident in your ability to lead and maintain quality conversations with your date, then you might want to intentionally choose dates that score lower on this scale. A few of the dates (like playing pool or people watching) are intentionally included in the book so that you can really let your personality shine through.

Cost Effective

Cost effectiveness speaks to how inexpensive the date is to pull off. Again, every date included in this book is intentionally inexpensive, but for those who are extra budget conscious, this parameter points you in the direction of which dates are lower-cost to zero-cost.

Brag-Worthiness

And finally, brag worthiness. This parameter basically measures the likelihood that your date will brag about this to her friends and family afterward.

Was it awe-inspiring, epic, and romantic? Then that date would rate a five out of five.

And now that you know the foundation for what makes a date powerful, let's get right into the fifty dates!

Activity Dates

1. Rock Climbing

5 star system

- Physical intimacy potential 1/5
- Emotional intimacy potential 4/5
- Conversational ease 4/5
- Cost Effective 5/5
- Brag-worthiness 4/5

The Fine Print

Get your heart rates pumping with this adrenaline-inducing date! Whether you want to start your relationship with some massive bragging points, or inject some energy into your lifeless long-term relationship, this one is an awesome catch-all date. Most major cities and suburbs have some sort of indoor climbing gym and the equipment rentals are usually cheap. Many gyms even have a discount for first-timers if you're new to climbing.

The Built-In Benefits

It is scientifically proven that people bond to others when going through any activity that makes their adrenaline surge. That means that this daredevil date packs a huge punch in the emotional connection department! If neither of you have gone rock climbing before, even better. It's also quite unique so many women haven't gone rock climbing before in any context, and almost certainly not on a date.

You will likely be controlling the rope for each other as you scale walls, which builds trust and comfort between the two of you. That being said, make sure that, halfway through the date, you suddenly pretend that you're going to drop her while you are lowering her, only to have her drop a foot or so. That usually gets you a playful smack on the arm once she is firmly planted on the ground. Another way to initiate touch on your date is to give her a hug or kiss as soon as she touches down from a good climb while her heart is still racing.

Troubleshooting

Make sure that you don't wear any clothing that is too tight. Also, avoid wearing any jewelry (and tell her to do the same) as it can get caught in the rope. Treat it like a fashionable workout… you want to be able to move comfortably in the clothes that you arrive in. Make sure that you let your date know to dress casually ahead of time. Nothing will kill the mood faster than having her show up in a dress and heels only to find out that she will be expected to climb multiple twenty-foot walls all the way to the ceiling. But don't worry too much as most indoor climbing gyms have shoes you can rent that are specifically for rock climbing.

2. Frisbee Golf (AKA Frolf)

5 star system

- Physical intimacy potential 1/5
- Emotional intimacy potential 4/5
- Conversational ease 2/5
- Cost Effective 5/5
- Brag-worthiness 2/5

The Fine Print

Grab a pair of frisbees and head to a "frolfing" course, or build your own. Frisbee golf is a fun, challenging, unique, and completely free date for you and your partner. If you have a frolfing course in your town, you might know that official frolf courses have 18 holes and are almost always 100% free. If you want to set up your own course, either head to a forest or public park that isn't too populated and designate the targets as you go. Certain examples of targets would be lampposts, trees, swing set poles, water fountains, etc.

The Built-In Benefits

This is one of the few dates in this book that can cost absolutely nothing. That doesn't mean that you can't combine it with another mini-date from this book to step up your game (e.g., picnic in the park). Any date that gets your competitive blood flowing generally creates a fun and playful dynamic between you and your date. You can even mischievously try to derail your partner's frisbee when she makes a throw- throw your frisbee at hers mid-flight! Make sure to do this only once or twice, and with a smile on your face, so she knows you aren't a jerk.

Troubleshooting

It's always good to pack a bag with any necessities (snacks, scorecard, pencil, umbrella, etc.) before you head out. Getting caught out in the rain while on the 9th hole of the game is anything but romantic (unless you kiss under said rain, then it's fully romantic). If she gets bored of the game halfway through, remain flexible and feel free to ditch it.

3. People Watching

5 star system

- Physical intimacy potential 4/5
- Emotional intimacy potential 4/5
- Conversational ease 3/5
- Cost Effective 5/5
- Brag-worthiness 3/5

The Fine Print

Just like it sounds, but less criminal. Go to the mall, a bookstore, or a public park and co-create stories about the people that you see. Take turns (either by the person or by the sentence) creating scenarios for the people around you. It is really quite fun and flirty; you also have the chance to tease each other in the process. Additionally, people watching tends to be a surprisingly effective way to get to know your date. She will tell creative stories about others that might actually say more about herself than about the people you are watching.

"See that anxious looking man over there? He was supposed to meet a blind date here. She said she would be wearing a red sweater… but he feels like he might have been stood up."

"See that couple walking around awkwardly? They just had a huge fight over how he never gets to watch his Saturday morning cartoons anymore and they are trying to save face now that they're in public."

"See that large group of guys in matching uniforms? They are professional golfers."

You get the picture. Encourage your date when she has really awesome ideas.

The Built-In Benefits

People watching makes for rapid rapport building. You also get to show off your creative muscles, and you get to do the whole activity sitting side by side, speaking quietly enough so that no one else can hear you. Intimate, free, and fun.

Troubleshooting

This date is low-risk, high reward. The only issue that might come up is that you find it hard to be 'creative' enough to keep the conversation going. When most guys think that they aren't being creative enough, what they really fear is that their ideas aren't clever or funny enough. Overcome this by realizing that simpler is always better than coming across as too try-hard. Don't aim for funny… you'll just get stuck in your head and you won't be present anymore. And if you do get stuck, let her lead the storytelling for a little while.

4. Kayaking And Packed Lunch Picnic

5 star system

- Physical intimacy potential 2/5
- Emotional intimacy potential 4/5
- Conversational ease 4/5
- Cost Effective 3/5
- Brag-worthiness 4/5

The Fine Print

If you live near any oceans or lakes, this date is sure to impress for those of you looking to enjoy the great outdoors. Kayak rentals are fairly inexpensive (often $10-25 for the pair) and you'll get to paddle around for a few hours. Pack a blanket and snacks in a backpack and leave it on shore for your arrival. What you don't get in the way of physical intimacy during the kayaking portion of your date, you can more than make up for when you're sitting on the picnic blanket later on in the day.

The Built-In Benefits

You don't have to do much talking if you have natural beauty around you as you are kayaking. The scenic beauty and physical exercise basically take care of the conversation for you. You will either be trying to catch your breath if you both paddle quickly, or you'll be silently admiring the beauty that surrounds you if you're drifting slowly.

Troubleshooting

You'll probably get tired after the first hour or two of kayaking; make sure you aren't stuck out at sea when your arm muscles start feeling sore. You won't want to paddle back to shore against the current! This inevitable exhaustion is where the picnic comes in. It's always good to refuel after a solid upper body workout.

5. Cooking Class

5 star system

- Physical intimacy potential 3/5
- Emotional intimacy potential 5/5
- Conversational ease 4/5
- Cost Effective 2/5
- Brag-worthiness 4/5

The Fine Print

Step out of your comfort zone with this unique date where you get to eat your art.

Many cooking classes offer affordable alternatives to full-price classes- discounted spots listed on an online group buying site, specials for online sign-up, or those with the option to buy your own ingredients ahead of time.

What if you're already a good cook? Then lead your own version of a cooking class! Buy the ingredients to prepare your favorite dish beforehand and spend a few hours with your date later on, co-creating your masterpiece meal.

The Built-In Benefits

This date has massive emotional intimacy potential because you get to play the adult version of 'house' while learning a new dish. It's inexpensive, cute, and builds rapport quickly.

Troubleshooting

Make sure you avoid any cooking classes that overcharge. Some classes can cost $80-100 per couple and are rarely worth the price. Worst case scenario, if you can't find any inexpensive class options, refer to the point above about making your own cooking class in-home. There are few things more attractive than a man who is egoless enough that he can be seen learning in front of his date and doesn't have to appear in control all of the time. Above all else, have fun with this!

6. Partnered Salsa Lessons

- 5 star system
- Physical intimacy potential 5/5
- Emotional intimacy potential 4/5
- Conversational ease 3/5
- Cost Effective 4/5

- Brag-worthiness 5/5

The Fine Print

This is easily one of the best dates for physical intimacy in this entire book and is always a sure way to heat up the passion in your relationship. Partnered salsa lessons are spreading like wildfire across major cities currently so it's never been easier to find a location to learn the dance. Often as cheap as $10-20 per couple for an evening's worth of entertainment, you really can't go wrong with this date.

The Built-In Benefits

Excessive physical closeness and emotional intimacy? Check. Inexpensive? Check. An easy excuse to be pressed up against your attractive date all night? Checkmate.

Troubleshooting

If you have two left feet when it comes to dancing, you might want to drop by a class or two on your own before you brave this one in a date situation. You will only have as much fun as you can feel confident. Most women love a man who can dance (and lead) effectively. As always, even if you are a hopeless dancer, the instructors are used to your kind walking through their doors. They should be able to make it simple enough that even the most dismal dancer can woo his partner effectively.

7. Yoga

5 star system

- Physical intimacy potential 1/5
- Emotional intimacy potential 3/5
- Conversational ease 4/5
- Cost Effective 4/5
- Brag-worthiness 2/5

The Fine Print

Think this date is a bit of a stretch? Not on your wallet! This active but calming date is great for those who are a bit more nervous when it comes to keeping the conversation flowing. An instructor guides you through all of the poses verbally while others demonstrate. Not as flexible as you'd like to be? No worries. You get bonus points just for showing up and trying it out.

The Built-In Benefits

Lowered heart rates, highly cost effective, and a unique bonding experience make this date a success. Be sure your yoga mats are next to each other for that "Us vs. The World" dynamic that comes from sharing such an intimate practice.

Troubleshooting

DON'T stare at the other girls in the room (especially while in downward dog pose). Your date will know you're doing it and so will everyone else. DO covertly give your partner a light tap on the bum when people aren't looking. Secrecy is sexy.

8. Flying A Kite In A Park

5 star system

- Physical intimacy potential 1/5
- Emotional intimacy potential 3/5
- Conversational ease 4/5
- Cost Effective 5/5
- Brag-worthiness 3/5

The Fine Print

Remember how fun flying a kite was when you were seven years old? Guess what… it's still fun as an adult! Dig up your childhood kite from the basement and take it to a beautiful, wide-open space. Take turns with your date trying to get the kite in the air, and then attempt to make it do flips. Work up a light sweat running it around while reconnecting with your inner child.

The Built-In Benefits

It's fun, brag-worthy, and does most of the conversational work for you. It also takes teamwork and patience to get the kite into the air, which is great for bonding.

Troubleshooting

Watch out for trees and power lines! Also, avoid days that call for lightning storms.

9. Chocolate Factory/Cheese Factory/Wine Tour/Brewery Tour

5 star system

- Physical intimacy potential 1/5
- Emotional intimacy potential 3/5
- Conversational ease 5/5
- Cost Effective 4/5
- Brag-worthiness 4/5

The Fine Print

A guided tour of any running food factory or beer/wine operation is great for the suitors that don't want to do the heavy lifting conversationally. Learn, be entertained, and indulge your tastebuds in this budget-friendly adventure. We are evolutionarily programmed to trust people that we eat and drink with so this date connects you with your partner on a deeper level.

The Built-In Benefits

Often cheap, sometimes free, and always awesome. It also scores high on the uniqueness factor as many people have never done these types of events in their hometown.

Troubleshooting

Don't overindulge in the cheese factory samples to avoid a sore stomach, and avoid over-imbibing in the wine or beer to avoid a nasty hangover. Some brewery and vineyard tours can be quite generous with their tastings so make sure that you don't get too drunk off their generosity.

10. Mini-Golf

5 star system

- Physical intimacy potential 4/5
- Emotional intimacy potential 3/5
- Conversational ease 5/5
- Cost Effective 5/5
- Brag-worthiness 4/5

The Fine Print

This old-school date is brought back with a competitive twist. Miniature golf is always fun- no matter how long it's been since you picked up a club. Set up a playful competition between the two of you and decide who gets what depending on who wins. Examples could be things like, "The winner gets treated to ice cream afterwards," "Whoever loses has to fake a British accent as they return the golf clubs," etc.

The Built-In Benefits

You really can't go wrong with this one. It ranks highly across the board and is always a fun and simple date. It works equally well as a first date as it does in the context of a long-term relationship. Also, no matter what stage you're in, a slight bit of playful 'cheating' is always welcome. Tap her ball in when it's an obviously close call with a "I didn't see that" expression on your face.

Troubleshooting

If you or your date needs a redo, let it slide. This date isn't an actual competition as much as it is an excuse to 'help her' with her golf swing. And if it turns out she's an A-game golfer? No sweat! Put your ego aside and let her mop the floor with you.

11. Go Ice-Skating

5 star system

- Physical intimacy potential 5/5
- Emotional intimacy potential 4/5
- Conversational ease 3/5
- Cost Effective 4/5
- Brag-worthiness 4/5

The Fine Print

An old classic resurrected. Grab some rental skates, hot chocolate, and hit the rink! This date is one of the few that people might have gone on when they were in their teens, and then let it slide for no reason other than sheer laziness. So find a local rink (indoor or outdoor), strap on some skates, and get gliding.

The Built-In Benefits

Ice skating is a fantastic way to build a connection. It has tons of opportunities for hand-holding and physical intimacy, and is a massively good value. Many ice rinks let you skate in the open-rink hours for under $10 (skate rentals included).

Troubleshooting

Is she especially Bambi-like on the ice? Make sure to stay close to her, hold her hand, or let her grip your forearm as a precautionary measure. Is she getting cold after your first half hour of ice-skating? Head to the lobby for some hot chocolate.

12. Shooting Range

5 star system

- Physical intimacy potential 2/5
- Emotional intimacy potential 4/5
- Conversational ease 4/5
- Cost Effective 3/5
- Brag-worthiness 5/5

The Fine Print

Head to the shooting range and try your hand at some target practice. Neither one of you has ever held a gun before? Don't worry about it. There are always copious amounts of staff at these places to give you a thorough run-down of gun slinging protocol.

The Built-In Benefits

Nothing makes your adrenaline soar like firing a gun for the first time (especially with a cute date at your side). You can also make a bet (see #10, mini-golf date for examples) for whoever gets the best shots on their target.

Troubleshooting

To be honest, this date is much more low-risk than it may seem. You are in a controlled environment with trained staff around you. Your conversations will easily flow (when shots aren't being fired) because your adrenaline will be coursing through your blood after the first round of gunfire.

13. Karaoke

5 star system

- Physical intimacy potential 3/5
- Emotional intimacy potential 5/5
- Conversational ease 5/5
- Cost Effective 4/5
- Brag-worthiness 4/5

The Fine Print

Nothing says adorable fun like singing off-key boy-band songs to each other in public. This date takes some courage but it is always good for a laugh. You can either do karaoke in a public bar (in which case, the cost is just whatever you end up eating/drinking) or you can rent a private room with friends for a couple of hours. Skim through the provided songbook, grab some drinks, and write down your song selection. Bonus points for songs that are partnered duets.

The Built-In Benefits

As with a few of the other activity dates, karaoke allows you and your date to bond over the adrenaline rush of putting yourself out there. If you've never done karaoke before, you truly don't know what you're missing. Give it a shot!

Troubleshooting

Are you an absolutely terrible singer? Even better! Karaoke is NOT about talent. It is about having fun! That goes for your song choice too. Should you pick the song that shows off your vocal range or the song that will be a ridiculous laugh-worthy joke? In karaoke, humor impresses over talent every time… so have fun with it!

14. Basketball

5 star system

- Physical intimacy potential 2/5
- Emotional intimacy potential 3/5
- Conversational ease 4/5
- Cost Effective 5/5
- Brag-worthiness 2/5

The Fine Print

Grab a basketball and go to your local public courts. Whether you're a beginner or a Harlem Globetrotter, this date is a slam-dunk. Pack some snacks and homemade sports drinks.

The Built-In Benefits

This date is extremely inexpensive, gets both your heart rates up, and has the potential for playful competition. What's not to like?

Troubleshooting

Make sure you tell your date in advance to wear running shoes and comfortable clothing. Is she utterly hopeless at the sport? No worries… feel free to modify the rules of the game. Above all else, HAVE FUN! Did she take four steps without dribbling? Don't worry about it. Relax the rules and make sure you're both enjoying yourselves.

15. Tandem Biking

5 star system

- Physical intimacy potential 4/5
- Emotional intimacy potential 5/5
- Conversational ease 3/5
- Cost Effective 5/5
- Brag-worthiness 5/5

The Fine Print

Rent and ride a tandem bike together around a scenic part of your town. It scores highly on the dorky scale but these kinds of dates are always the easiest to laugh about.

The Built-In Benefits

Have you ever seen two people trying to sync up getting onto a tandem bike? There is a 99% chance that it looked awkward. That is why this is a great idea for a date. It's slightly awkward at the beginning, filled with laughter, and then ends with you syncing up perfectly. And in the end, isn't that the way that every successful date goes

Troubleshooting

Want to be seen as the leader of the date? Sit up front and steer. Want to be in a position to initiate more touch and let your partner navigate? Take the back seat and be the driving force of your collective momentum. Feel free to covertly pack some bandages in your back pocket just in case somebody scrapes a knee.

16. Driving Range

5 star system

- Physical intimacy potential 3/5
- Emotional intimacy potential 2/5
- Conversational ease 5/5
- Cost 5/5
- Brag-worthiness 3/5

The Fine Print

Hit the driving range to lob some balls into the stratosphere. Hint: neither one of you has to be good for this date to be fun! After a few rounds, head to the clubhouse for a drink.

The Built-In Benefits

Another great date for those who don't want to do too much work conversationally. Buckets of golf balls and golf club rentals are pretty cheap and can give you hours of entertainment. It's also fun to occasionally give your date some ridiculously terrible advice on how to hold the club or how to stand. (And of course, make sure your terrible advice is *obviously* terrible.)

Troubleshooting

The best thing about the driving range is that you're only as good as your last shot- so don't worry about making it into a competition. Worst-case scenario, one of you accidentally throws your golf club into the water hazard in an overeager swing and a staff member has to give you a replacement. As always, relax… have fun… and enjoy the process.

17. Whale Watching

5 star system

- Physical intimacy potential 5/5
- Emotional intimacy potential 5/5
- Conversational ease 4/5
- Cost 3/5
- Brag-worthiness 5/5

The Fine Print

If you live near the ocean, go on a whale-watching cruise. When you see a whale, make sure you say something like, 'Wow, Shamu has really let himself go.' Last minute tickets are often under $20 per person so keep your eyes peeled for spots on local websites.

The Built-In Benefits

The serenity of the ocean, the breathtaking views, and the anticipation of seeing one of the world's largest creatures all make for an exciting and inexpensive date. If there is a decent amount of sea-breeze you can even wrap up in each other's arms for warmth. No matter what the weather conditions are, this date scores major bonus point in the physical and emotional intimacy departments because you get to feel like you're searching for buried treasure together.

Troubleshooting

The potential hazards for this date are seasickness (pack anti-nausea medicine if you think you or your date will be prone to this), sea spray from the water (bring a jacket), and hunger (pack snacks). Even if you don't see any whales or sea life, you get a beautiful and relaxing day out on the water.

Romantic Date Structures

18. Art Night-In

5 star system

- Physical intimacy potential 3/5
- Emotional intimacy potential 5/5
- Conversational ease 5/5
- Cost 3/5
- Brag-worthiness 5/5

The Fine Print

A creative date where you buy a canvas or two, some basic coloured kid's paint, and paint together in your house (with newspaper on the ground). A couple bottles of red or white wine will help to get the creativity flowing.

The Built-In Benefits

Everyone has a creative side! In most cultures, artistic expression is missing from daily living. This is a great way to infuse some creative juices back into your love life. Creativity also reawakens parts of your mind that can feel somewhat dormant when they are underused… so this date has the added benefit of making you both a little smarter.

Troubleshooting

Can't think of what to paint? Start with anything. Anything at all. Start with a red stop sign. Start by poking a hole through the painting. Start by splattering random paint on the canvas. Just start making a mess and your creative mind will take over from there.

19. Spanish Themed Night-In

5 star system

- Physical intimacy potential 4/5
- Emotional intimacy potential 5/5
- Conversational ease 5/5
- Cost 2/5
- Brag-worthiness 5/5

The Fine Print

Make a sensually driven evening out of spanish guitar music on the speakers, a bottle of red wine, and some small samples of fine cheeses and meats. Dim lights and candles work well in this setting.

The Built-In Benefits

Sensuality, reawakened senses, and the appreciation of a beautiful culture make for one romantic evening.

The conversation will flow as you both slip into your sensuous Spanish alter-egos while sipping red wine. When the music is playing and the wine is flowing, make sure you take your partner's hand and initiate a slow-motion slow dance in the middle of the kitchen. Lots of eye contact and mental presence are a must. Finally, there's very little pressure to do much work conversationally on this date. Let the stillness ride out and allow the music to do the talking.

Troubleshooting

For the meats, cheeses, or any other delicacies you choose to serve, the rule is always quality over quantity. Regardless of your budget, you want the highest quality morsels of food in small portions. On this date, less is more.

20. Around-The-House "Drive-In" Movie

5 star system

- Physical intimacy potential 5/5
- Emotional intimacy potential 4/5
- Conversational ease 5/5
- Cost 5/5
- Brag-worthiness 5/5

The Fine Print

Grab the biggest, thickest blanket you can find, head out to the yard and watch a movie outdoors. With digital projector, hot chocolate, and some popcorn in your arsenal, this date is a one-way ticket to bragging rights. It takes some planning, but if you have a yard with access to electricity, this date is pure magic.

The Built-In Benefits

Where do I even begin? This date rates as a 5 star across the board (except for emotional intimacy at a 4/5 because the movie will be doing most of the talking) and for good reason. Unless you live in a climate where it's near freezing out year round, this date is an absolute ace-in-the-hole.

Troubleshooting

If you do live in a colder climate, either double up on the blankets and layers, or set up the exact same date within the confines of a tent. Don't have a digital projector? Check with your friends (many people own one these days) or rent one inexpensively from a film production rental store in your town.

21. The Secret Envelope Date Structure

5 star system

- Physical intimacy potential N/A
- Emotional intimacy potential N/A
- Conversational ease N/A
- Cost N/A
- Brag-worthiness 5/5

The Fine Print

Hand her three envelopes with different possible dates for the night- insist that she can only pick one, and then you will be doing that date together. The other two are scrapped and you don't mention them again. This shows uber-preparedness. Pro tip: even if all three of the cards say the same thing, she'll never know… but that's our little secret. Short on three date ideas? Search through the other 49 ideas in this book!

The Built-In Benefits

The epitome of romance! Anticipation, preparedness, and fate all combine to make for an amazing pre-date jolt of romantic lightning.

Troubleshooting

The only thing that could go wrong is if you choose to write the same thing on all three cards and she somehow sees the other two cards. The best way to avoid this? Don't take the easy way out. Plan three stellar, inexpensive dates from the pages of this book and let the journey unfold.

22. Sunrise Surprise

5 star system

- Physical intimacy potential 3/5
- Emotional intimacy potential 5/5
- Conversational ease 4/5
- Cost 5/5
- Brag-worthiness 5/5

The Fine Print

If you live near somewhere that has a beautiful lookout and isn't too difficult to get to, pick up your date early in the morning and drive/hike to the location. Get to the top of the lookout point by sunrise and eat a pre-packed breakfast.

The Built-In Benefits

You get to show your outdoorsy side, get some exercise, and share a very unique and beautiful experience. This ultra-cheap date rates highly on the brag-o-meter for good reason.

Troubleshooting

She isn't much of a hiker? That's fine. Take your time, and get to the top at her pace. Even if you get to the top half an hour after sunrise, it's still fun to watch the world wake up. Make sure to pack ample snacks, water, and a camera to capture the memory.

23. Runway Rendezvous

5 star system

- Physical intimacy potential 5/5
- Emotional intimacy potential 4/5
- Conversational ease 2/5
- Cost 5/5
- Brag-worthiness 3/5

The Fine Print

Drive out to your local airport and park near the landing strip (OFF the runway). Bring a blanket for the hood of the car (and a spare one in case it gets chilly). Lie back and watch the planes take off and land. Don't forget to bring snacks! Though not every city has this opportunity available, it can be well worth the drive to your nearest runway.

The Built-In Benefits

Physical intimacy, uniqueness, and a very new perspective on the world all come with this fantastic date. This is one of the several dates in this book that the vast majority of people have never experienced. This is also one of the most cost effective dates in this book. Aside from having a full tank of gas, price of admission is free and the food and beverages are up to your personal taste.

Troubleshooting

Make sure you scope out the location before you set the date. Nothing kills the mood faster than realizing that the place at which you assumed you would park is actually closed or off-limits to the public. Pack snacks, extra blankets for the colder seasons, and some of your favorite drinks to enjoy the show.

24. See A Drive-In Movie

5 star system

- Physical intimacy potential 4/5
- Emotional intimacy potential 3/5
- Conversational ease 5/5
- Cost 3/5
- Brag-worthiness 3/5

The Fine Print

Gas up the car, head out to the suburbs, and catch a movie at an old-fashioned drive-in theatre while you still can.

The Built-In Benefits

What's old is new again! The retro feel is always appreciated. The conversation is taken care of you while you kick back and enjoy the film together. And if the windows end up getting steamy from your hot and heavy physical intimacy, who cares? The movie wasn't THAT good anyways...

Troubleshooting

Your city doesn't have a drive-in theatre any more? Not a problem. Check out date #20 to do it yourself!

25. Outdoors Table For Two

5 star system

- Physical intimacy potential 4/5
- Emotional intimacy potential 5/5

- Conversational ease 4/5
- Cost 3/5
- Brag-worthiness 5/5

The Fine Print

This date takes a bit more planning but is great for people in long-term relationships. Have a close mutual friend set up a small table near a beautiful location (ocean, river, lake, or other easily-accessed lookout point) and serve you both a simple dinner. Make sure to plan to include the tablecloth, food, and wine.

The Built-In Benefits

This date shows off your ability to lead and be chivalrous. It also demonstrates to your partner that you still want to woo her. With a healthy dose of forethought, this romantic date is hard to mess up and is massively brag-worthy.

Troubleshooting

I've said it before and I'll say it again… planning, planning, and more planning! Plan ahead as much as you can and this date will be smooth sailing. You'll want to arrive to the table with almost everything already set up. Either you or your friend should prepare the table, tablecloth, cutlery, and plates before you and your partner arrive. Have all of your backup supplies in your car if you plan on driving to the location. A sample list of backup supplies to bring: wine, wine opener, candles, matches, flowers, small blankets, and something to play music for you and your date.

26. Book Store/Library Date

5 star system

- Physical intimacy potential 3/5
- Emotional intimacy potential 4/5
- Conversational ease 5/5
- Cost 5/5
- Brag-worthiness 2/5

The Fine Print

Go to a local bookstore or library and sit in your favourite section for a couple of hours. Take turns picking books from the shelf and reading to each other. The bigger the bookstore, the less they will care that you're there. This works surprisingly well as a both a first date and as a date for those in long-term relationships.

The Built-In Benefits

No matter what stage you're in, this date will allow you to learn more about your partner very quickly. The conversation takes care of itself since you have endless subject matter right at your fingertips. You can also let your date choose which section she wants to sit in. Who knows… maybe you like reading educational texts and she enjoys fantasy books. Be open to the process and see what you discover about each other.

Troubleshooting

Depending on the attention spans of both you and your partner, this date may start to feel stale after a couple of hours. Luckily, due to its massive cost-effectiveness, you can always tack on another one of the dates mentioned in this book to follow.

27. Hot-Air Balloon/Helicopter Sightseeing

5 star system

- Physical intimacy potential 4/5
- Emotional intimacy potential 5/5
- Conversational ease 5/5
- Cost 2/5
- Brag-worthiness 5/5

The Fine Print

Let your sense of adventure take off to new heights on this awesome, brag-worthy date. Keep a look out on group buying websites to find hot-air balloon or helicopter sightseeing rides. You can sometimes find rates for two for under $40.

The Built-In Benefits

The danger of the date allows you and your partner to quickly bond, while the view will take your breath away. This one also scores highly on brag-worthiness for obvious reasons. After this date, your bucket list will definitely be shorter.

Troubleshooting

If you or your partner are known for having a petrifying fear of heights, then this date probably isn't for you. If you're only mildly hesitant about partaking in this thrill-ride, I strongly recommend it. The stunning pay-off is well worth the erratic heartbeats and quickened pulses.

Traditional Dates With A Spin

28. Billiards

5 star system

- Physical intimacy potential 5/5
- Emotional intimacy potential 3/5
- Conversational ease 5/5
- Cost 4/5
- Brag-worthiness 2/5

The Fine Print

When was the last time you played pool? A fun way to raise the stakes while playing pool is to attach a bet to it. Set the parameters before your first break. I've found that "best 2 out of 3" is a sweet spot that works well for dates. It's long enough that you get to build an emotional connection, and short enough that neither of you gets bored.

The Built-In Benefits

The date is both playful and competitive, and the conversational flow will mostly take care of itself. This date is a breeze! If she needs help lining up her next shot, who are you to say no? This date rates highly on the physical intimacy potential because of this- you have the ability to be quite close to her, one hand on her waist and the other on the cue. You can also playfully tease your date by nudging her pool cue just before she takes a shot.

Troubleshooting

The only troubleshooting you might have is if you have trouble shooting. So don't go on this date if you are terrible at pool. Can't think of what to set as the prize if one of you wins? Some of my favorites have been 1) you have to go two-for-one shots the rest of the night, 2) she has to fake a British accent while ordering the next round, and 3) walk with a limp for the next hour. Get creative and have fun with it. Make it your own.

29. Look Out!

- 5 star system
- Physical intimacy potential 5/5
- Emotional intimacy potential 4/5
- Conversational ease 3/5
- Cost 5/5
- Brag-worthiness 5/5

The Fine Print

Imagine this… picking up your date and driving out to the most scenic nighttime look out point that you can find. Secretly stowed away in the back seat are a thermos filled with hot chocolate, a battery-operated music player, and blankets.

The Built-In Benefits

This date is romantic, intimate, unique, and one of my personal favourites. As long as you have SOME beautiful look out (whether you're looking out over the city, water or sky, it really doesn't matter), this date is an absolute winner. It works equally well as a first date and as a five-hundredth date.

Troubleshooting

The only thing that has ever gone wrong with this date for me in the past was back when I was driving a 1984 Oldsmobile. I didn't account for the fact that playing the radio for hours while the engine was off was going to drain the battery. So after an amazing and romantic five hours of beautiful scenery, the car wouldn't start. Luckily, I was able to use my cell phone to call a friend to come pick us up. Moral of the story? Make sure you don’t use your car battery when you attempt this date! Or at least have a cell phone on you (on silent mode) just in case.

30. Watching an amateur stand-up comedy night

5 star system

- Physical intimacy potential 2/5
- Emotional intimacy potential 2/5
- Conversational ease 5/5
- Cost 5/5
- Brag-worthiness 3/5

The Fine Print

The vast majority of venues that host stand-up comedy have an "amateur night" where new up-and-coming comedians hone their performing chops. The truth is that most of them are absolutely terrible... but that's half the fun! How does the saying go? Oh right, "The couple that cringes together, stays together."

The Built-In Benefits

Lots of laughs!

Troubleshooting

It's bound to happen that you'll go to an amateur night and NONE of the comedians are any good. You and your date sit there making uncomfortable faces at each other. In this scenario, the only way out is by using the awkwardness as the catalyst for your own sense of humor. Nothing shows social intelligence like letting your date know that the performers aren't up to snuff. Whatever you decide to do after the comedy portion of your date, use references from the performers as callback humor.

31. Seeing A Live Dance Performance

5 star system

- Physical intimacy potential 2/5
- Emotional intimacy potential 3/5
- Conversational ease 5/5
- Cost 5/5
- Brag-worthiness 4/5

The Fine Print

Enjoy the arts together by taking in a passionate night of dancing. Think you have two left feet? Not a problem. You'll be watching the performers, not joining them. Tip: Dance styles like flamenco, salsa, and ballroom all have sensual vibes and are generally much more fun to watch than ballet.

The Built-In Benefits

Few things make a woman's heart race more than watching passionate performers working within their genius. The talent and intensity of the aforementioned dance styles also add an edgy vibe to your date.

Troubleshooting

Two things could make this date go south in a hurry… 1) you don't enjoy the performance because you're just doing this for her, and 2) you both don't enjoy the performance because the dancers aren't very good. Take care of the first problem by really letting yourself go to the evening. Allow yourself to take in the beauty and grace of the dancers. Observe their passion with an open mind. She will be able to tell if you're not into it and it could very well ruin the night for her… so make yourself care! Don't let the second issue arise; it is easily taken care of if you scope out the venue beforehand. Do the performers seem like they love their craft? Then it's a winner. Do they seem like they're just going through the motions and they couldn't care less? Time to find another venue.

32. Watching A Live Theatre Performance Or Improvisational Comedy Show

5 star system

- Physical intimacy potential 2/5
- Emotional intimacy potential 4/5
- Conversational ease 5/5
- Cost 5/5
- Brag-worthiness 2/5

The Fine Print

Search your local newspaper or online directory for any amateur or professional theatre groups that regularly put shows on in your area. They are surprisingly engaging and, if you go the improv route, you might even end up onstage.

The Built-In Benefits

The conversation is taken care of for you on this entertaining date. Bonus: you get to support your local arts economy.

Troubleshooting

If you go see a show and your relationship is young, make sure it's something lighthearted and fun. Nothing kills the mood like a dark, depressing drama on the first date.

33. Go Bowling

5 star system

- Physical intimacy potential 3/5
- Emotional intimacy potential 3/5
- Conversational ease 4/5
- Cost 4/5
- Brag-worthiness 3/5

The Fine Print

What was fun when you were six years old is still fun now! Share a milkshake- one glass, two straws- if you want to be old-fashioned (or indulge in a pitcher of beer, whichever appeals more to you and your date).

The Built-In Benefits

It's playful, competitive, interactive, and a fun challenge to shake up the old routine. You also get to wear silly shoes that look like clowns designed them.

Troubleshooting

Unless you drop the ball on your own foot, I really can't imagine much going wrong with this date. It's a classic for a reason!

34. Art Gallery/Science Centre

5 star system

- Physical intimacy potential 2/5
- Emotional intimacy potential 3/5
- Conversational ease 5/5
- Cost 5/5
- Brag-worthiness 4/5

The Fine Print

Search online to find your local science centre or art gallery. Many of these venues have an adults only night once a month, often with free admission, where you can sip wine and interact with the exhibits.

The Built-In Benefits

Get caught up on culture, take in visual art, and feel fancy as you sip your wine. Or in the science centre example, get your hands messy, make your hair stand on end with static electricity generators, and learn about how the world works together.

Troubleshooting

For most people, these dates are a once-in-a-while kind of deal… but they can be truly fascinating if you let your inner child run free. So embrace the process and enjoy it.

35. Day Time Symphony Orchestra

5 star system

- Physical intimacy potential 2/5
- Emotional intimacy potential 3/5
- Conversational ease 5/5
- Cost 4/5
- Brag-worthiness 5/5

The Fine Print

Many major cities have symphony performances in the daytime. Matinee shows are inexpensive, less crowded, and have a bunch of cute old people that you can make up stories about to each other.

The Built-In Benefits

Culture, beauty, and refinement all wrapped up in a neat little package. If this date idea speaks to you, I'd definitely recommending giving it a try.

Troubleshooting

The only downside to this date is the physical intimacy potential. Unless you don't mind grandma and grandpa seeing you and your date canoodling, it's a bit hard to do much more than hold hands during this date. Fortunately, it scores quite well across the board and is definitely brag-worthy. Just wait until her friends hear about how classy you both are!

Food-Based Dates

36. Fondue

5 star system

- Physical intimacy potential 3/5
- Emotional intimacy potential 5/5
- Conversational ease 4/5
- Cost 4/5
- Brag-worthiness 5/5

The Fine Print

Melt a big load of chocolate in a crock pot and have various fruits, marshmallows, cake bits and brownie chunks prepared for dipping.

The Built-In Benefits

We are evolutionarily hardwired to trust those with whom we dine. This date is a quick way to bond, and access emotional intimacy with your partner. Plus, SO MUCH CHOCOLATE!

Troubleshooting
The calories add up quickly, but who's counting?

37. Finger Foods

5 star system

- Physical intimacy potential 3/5
- Emotional intimacy potential 5/5
- Conversational ease 4/5
- Cost 4/5
- Brag-worthiness 5/5

The Fine Print

Make a finger-foods only night-in with share plates that you have put together ahead of time.

The Built-In Benefits

Bust out your inner chef and impress your date. Feeding each other is uber-romantic. And, for your date, being fed food that YOU made for her gets you even more bonus points.

Troubleshooting

Having trouble of thinking what to make? Creativity and originality are key to this date's success. I personally have gotten my best reactions from homemade Oreos, owl-shaped mini-sandwiches, feta-stuffed jalapenos, sun-dried tomato pesto rolls, and other classic appetizers with small twists. Think about what food you both generally like, and then consider fun or endearing tweaks to make those dishes bite-sized and relevant to your relationship.

38. Farmers Market

5 star system

- Physical intimacy potential 3/5
- Emotional intimacy potential 5/5
- Conversational ease 4/5
- Cost 4/5
- Brag-worthiness 4/5

The Fine Print

Take your date to your local farmers market and browse the high-quality and nutritious goods. Part two of this date is to make dinner together by mutually deciding what you could create out of your newly discovered ingredients.

The Built-In Benefits

Tasty, romantic, and a fun team project. If you've never been to a farmers market before, you're seriously missing out. There are often loads of samples for you to try and the prices are usually unbeatable.

Troubleshooting

The farmers market won't let you down so the only problem that could arise would be indecisiveness. If your date doesn't have a strong preference for what to eat, feel free to take the lead and offer up a suggestion. And if you don't consider yourself a good cook? Dishes like casseroles, stir-fries, and chilies often hide a lot of the little mistakes. So pick up the ingredients, experiment, and enjoy your meal!

Embrace Your Inner Child!

39. Play in the park

5 star system

- Physical intimacy potential 3/5
- Emotional intimacy potential 4/5
- Conversational ease 4/5
- Cost 5/5
- Brag-worthiness 5/5

The Fine Print

An old classic that deserves being brought back from your childhood. I have yet to meet a woman that disliked getting on a swing and being pushed. Most women used to spend countless hours playing in the park when they were little girls. This date brings back childhood memories for both of you.

The Built-In Benefits

Fresh air, sunshine, and getting to be a kid again, if only for a little while, are all perks for this date. Don't be afraid to reconnect with your inner child for a few hours. Play on the slide, jump on a teeter-totter or challenge your date to a game of tag. This date will bring lots of laughs, in addition to allowing you to either create or strengthen your emotional connection.

Troubleshooting

Make sure you tell your date to dress casually. Nothing will ruin a day at the park more than the wrong shoes and an inappropriate outfit. If you want to blow her away with a little romance, tie in a picnic to this occasion and you'll show her you can have a great time anywhere.

40. Indoor Picnic

5 star system

- Physical intimacy potential 4/5
- Emotional intimacy potential 4/5
- Conversational ease 3/5
- Cost 5/5
- Brag-worthiness 5/5

The Fine Print

This one works well for those less-than-beautiful days of weather. Spread a large blanket on the floor of your kitchen and eat your picnic on it. Bonus points if the kitchen table is only a few feet away from you.

The Built-In Benefits

Unique, intimate, and no need to call ahead to make a reservation.

Troubleshooting

Make sure you don't use a blanket that wouldn't be able to handle getting food spilled on it. (Some blankets are *so* high maintenance.)

41. Build A Fort Together

5 star system

- Physical intimacy potential 5/5
- Emotional intimacy potential 4/5
- Conversational ease 3/5
- Cost 5/5
- Brag-worthiness 5/5

The Fine Print

No, I'm not joking. This date has worked both for my clients and for me so many times that I've lost count. In addition to making a home-cooked meal for your date, build a fully functioning fort out of mattresses, pillows, blankets and whatever else you can find lying around that will be comfortable to cuddle in when it eventually collapses.

The Built-In Benefits

Tied with tandem biking as the dorkiest date in the book, this one has adorable written all over it. This date is what you make of it. And, like a few of the other dates, because it has zero cost attached to it, feel free to add one of the other date ideas on top of this as a bonus.

Troubleshooting

If this date sounds like something you could pull off, go for it! Fun is contagious and she will enjoy herself too. Just make sure that you sell it like you care. "We're going to build a FORT! Let's round up all of the blankets we can find and make something seriously epic."

42. Sexy Jenga!

5 star system

- Physical intimacy potential 5/5
- Emotional intimacy potential 5/5
- Conversational ease 5/5
- Cost 5/5
- Brag-worthiness 5/5

The Fine Print

It's basically truth or dare with Jenga blocks that you tailor to your relationship. Write a personalized sexy message, command, or intimate question on each stacking block. Whichever block is pulled by either you or your date, you must read the message out loud, and then do what the block says.

The Built-In Benefits

This is the only date that scores as an enthusiastic five out of five across the whole scoreboard. It's free, brag-worthy, takes care of the conversation for you, and definitely gets you physically and emotionally closer to each other. No wonder so many of us played truth or dare in high school… apparently we were on to something!

Troubleshooting

Make sure the phones are turned off for this date, as it can get hot and heavy pretty quickly depending on what you have written on the blocks. Not the creative type? You don't have to write down all of your ideas in one sitting. Let them come to you over time and write them down on a list as they occur to you. Some sample ideas?

Take off one article of clothing that isn't your socks or jewelry. Describe your first kiss. Nibble your partner's earlobe for thirty seconds. Describe your ultimate sexual fantasy. Look deeply into your partner's eyes for thirty seconds. Kiss the body part on your partner that you love the most for thirty seconds.

This date is as sexy or as tame as you want to make it. Enjoy!

43. See A Local Sporting Event

5 star system

- Physical intimacy potential 4/5
- Emotional intimacy potential 4/5
- Conversational ease 5/5
- Cost 3/5
- Brag-worthiness 4/5

The Fine Print

Whether at the professional or amateur level, many tickets to baseball/ hockey/ soccer games are surprisingly inexpensive. Hit the internet to check out the time table of upcoming events at your local arenas. If you go to an amateur level game, the players are often more enthusiastic and hungrier for attention because they want to stand out to get drafted.

The Built-In Benefits

Delicious snacks, conversational ease, and most importantly, big foam fingers!

Troubleshooting

Not every woman will be ecstatic about going to a live sporting event, so make sure this date is something that you would both be into before you buy the tickets. If you're going to a hockey game or outdoor event, make sure to bring an extra layer just in case your date gets cold.

44. Planetarium

5 star system

- Physical intimacy potential 3/5
- Emotional intimacy potential 3/5
- Conversational ease 5/5
- Cost 4/5
- Brag-worthiness 3/5

The Fine Print

Visit a planetarium together (bonus points if they have cool laser shows). Like the art gallery and science centre date (#34), planetariums are educational and often have adults only evenings.

The Built-In Benefits

Educational, inexpensive, and the added bonus of being the only date during which you get to proudly announce, "I can see Uranus!" (I *had* to…)

Troubleshooting

What could go wrong while watching magical lasers being shot around the room? In my experience, absolutely nothing. I once took a date to see "Pink Floyd, Dark Side of the Moon" and we both found it exhilarating. This date is low maintenance and mentally engaging.

45. A Day At The Races

5 star system

- Physical intimacy potential 3/5
- Emotional intimacy potential 3/5
- Conversational ease 5/5
- Cost 4/5
- Brag-worthiness 4/5

The Fine Print

Go to a horse racing track and place make believe bets on the horses. Establish what each person wins if their picks win more races. Be sure to keep track to see who is victorious!

The Built-In Benefits

What animal does almost every child wish for? You guessed it, a pony (although puppies are a close second). I'm not sure what it is, but most girls I've met have had a fascination with horses, and this date totally plays into that. On top of that, you can make some fun bets. Whether you are betting for real money or not, the excitement and anticipation of waiting for your horse to win is surprisingly fun. This date works especially well if neither of you have ever been to a racetrack before.

Troubleshooting

Worst-case scenario, her horses beat yours every time. What to do then? Pony up on the bet! Whatever you committed to doing before the race started, you have to do. See the pool bet date (#28) for a few starter ideas on what to bet each other.

46. Arcade

5 star system

- Physical intimacy potential 3/5
- Emotional intimacy potential 3/5
- Conversational ease 5/5
- Cost 4/5
- Brag-worthiness 4/5

The Fine Print

Go to the arcade and only play two-player games. This makes for a cheap, fun, and competitive date. Be sure that, if you're really good, you don't beat her too many times in a row. Allow her the chance to win every few games.

The Built-In Benefits

This date is good old-fashioned fun. Between pong, racing games, and Mortal Kombat, you have a plethora of options as to what kind of vibe the night will hold. You'll be surprised to see how far a $20 bill goes in creating memories for the two of you.

Troubleshooting

If your date is terrible at playing video games, ease off a little in the skill department. I have found this date to be a lot of fun for about an hour, but then you want to have a second part to the date. In my experience, it's a rare woman who would thoroughly enjoy only playing video games for four or more hours.

47. Sun-Date

5 star system

- Physical intimacy potential 2/5
- Emotional intimacy potential 3/5
- Conversational ease 5/5
- Cost 3/5
- Brag-worthiness 4/5

The Fine Print

After wrapping up one of these other super cheap date ideas (like playing basketball together, #14), head to your kitchen and create the most elaborate ice cream sundaes you both can imagine. Have at least ten different ingredients prepared to use. I'd suggest a few different flavors of ice cream, caramel, bananas, marshmallows, chocolate chips, rainbow sprinkles, cherries, peaches, hot fudge, maple syrup, nuts and whatever else your sweet tooth might crave.

The Built-In Benefits

Indulge in decadence! This delicious date brings you both back to your senses.

Troubleshooting

This date is self-explanatory and low-risk… unless you are on a diet.

48. Go-Karting

5 star system

- Physical intimacy potential 1/5
- Emotional intimacy potential 3/5
- Conversational ease 4/5
- Cost 5/5
- Brag-worthiness 5/5

The Fine Print

Speed across the finish line in this adrenaline-pumping date.

The Built-In Benefits

When was the last time you felt the wind in your hair? Low-cost, low-risk, and high octane… this date brings out the speed demon in everyone.

Troubleshooting

Most go-karting courses don't let you bump into each other, and for good reason. If you accidentally hit the tire of your date, you could find yourself mounting her car unexpectedly! Best to keep your distance, go at a semi-reasonable pace, and allow the race to stay fairly neck-and-neck to keep the excitement alive.

Fancy Dates, Done Dirt Cheap

49. Home Spa

5 star system

- Physical intimacy potential 5/5
- Emotional intimacy potential 5/5
- Conversational ease 5/5
- Cost 4/5
- Brag-worthiness 5/5

The Fine Print

Bring the spa home with a handful of easy ingredients. Buy some Epsom salts, foot scrubbers, moisturizer, and massage oil for a quick and easy do-it-yourself spa day. Take turns giving each other pedicures and face massages. Nothing says intimacy like trusting someone to pamper you.

The Built-In Benefits

Almost a perfect score across the board. The physical and emotional intimacy are a given, and the brag-worthiness is through the roof on this one. I can hear her friends screaming now- "He did what? Jonathan, why don't YOU do that for me!?" Boyfriend… of… the year!

Troubleshooting

Not the best at giving massages? Go the extra mile and secretly take a massage course before you set this date up. Make sure you execute this date with the intention of being good at giving pleasure and relaxation, not getting. If it looks like you just bought massage oils so that you could benefit, this date will be going in a completely different (and not so great) direction.

50. Movie Marathon

5 star system

- Physical intimacy potential 5/5
- Emotional intimacy potential 3/5
- Conversational ease 5/5
- Cost 4/5
- Brag-worthiness 3/5

The Fine Print

Pick an awesome film trilogy or a season of a classic TV show that you both like and watch it all in one sitting. Don't forget the popcorn!

The Built-In Benefits

Low maintenance, lots of cuddling, and easy to set up. It works just as well for new and long-term relationships alike (but it's best to avoid this as a first date).

Troubleshooting

If you start to get bored after a few movies/episodes, than switch it up by going for a walk. Whether you walk around the block or just to the fridge, don't worry… I won't judge.

Frequently Asked Questions

Will she think I'm being cheap?

Resourcefulness is an attractive trait for a person of any income level. I once met a woman who gave me a clear example of this. She had dated two men in the past… 1) a rich guy who lived in the nicest area of town and treated his place like crap, and 2) a struggling artist with extremely limited resources that took care of all of his possessions with immaculate care and attention. She stated that guy #1 made thousands of dollars more a year than guy #2. She also said that when it came to choosing which lifestyle she found more attractive, guy #2 won by a landslide. Most quality women would share that mindset.

- What if the dorky ones are too dorky and she thinks I'm a little boy?

A real man can embrace his inner child in any given moment. If you are too concerned about how you will appear in your relationships then you will always live a sort of half-life. Let go of trying to please others simply to salvage your ego. For more on this, check out this blog post http://www.jordangrayconsulting.com/2013/02/strength-in-vulnerability/

- There are so many to choose from, where do I begin?

Just do one. Do whichever date that most speaks to you and your personality. Some of these will be outside of your comfort zone and that's totally fine. There's more than enough in here to get some monstrous momentum in your dating life.

By the way, if a lot of these dates seem fairly simple, that's because they are. Mastering a simple date and letting your character shine through is much more attractive than trying (and failing) to pull off an unnecessarily elaborate date. What would you rather have… a ridiculously delicious hot dog, or a steak and lobster combo that is dry, tough, and bitter? Remember: simple is better.

That's it for now...

I am currently compiling dates for a second edition of this book with all new dates so keep tabs on my website for updates. I also update my website (http://www.jordangrayconsulting.com/) weekly with new blog posts regarding masculinity, attraction, relationship management, emotional development, and sexuality.

Thanks for reading!

Jordan Gray

About the Author

#1 Amazon best-selling author, relationship coach, and jet-setting world traveler, Jordan Gray helps people remove their emotional blocks, and get into (and maintain) thriving intimate relationships.

His thoughts on modern dating and relationships have been featured in numerous print publications, and on radio and television broadcasts internationally.

In his relationship coaching practice, Jordan has worked with thousands of students over the past four years, and has more wedding invitations from his former clients than he can keep up with.

When he's not coaching clients or writing new books, Jordan loves to surf without a wetsuit, immerse himself in new cultures, and savor slow motion hang outs with his closest companions.

You can find his books on Amazon, and you can see more of his writing at www.jordangrayconsulting.com.

CPSIA information can be obtained
at www.ICGtesting.com
Printed in the USA
BVHW070613201218
536071BV00002B/614/P